I have never considered myself to be intelligent.
However I think a lot and write my thoughts
for the purpose of sharing and boosting
the readers' spirits

Possibly, this book of quotes will stir your
thoughts and cause you to smile a bit or even
act on what you read

**Wisdom finds no place to land
when the runway is paved with fools.**

**It does not have to be big to be effective.
Small changes can yield big results.**

**Problems, like weeds, will not go away
unless you prune them at the roots.**

Credibility Gap...
Lack of continuity between words and actions.

Appearance of doing good comes from
the mind.
The act of doing going comes from
the heart.

Ever notice how some people take recycling
too far...
like, reminding you over and over
what you did wrong?

**A genuine positive attitude
is molded
from clay of gratitude.**

**Some people book regular flights
to
the islands of negative thinking.**

**Some folks have more pounds to shed
before their character
finds its ideal weight.**

The portrait of true character is revealed when the paint of adversity dries.

Sometimes negative thoughts develop
as though
they were planted in Miracle Grow.

My eyesight is best when I'm standing.
My insight is best when I'm kneeling.

Children are like sponges that absorb
dirty water as easily as clean water.
Be sure your filters are changed regularly.

Trust

Fear Him...revere Him...stay near Him.

**Faith in God, coupled with daily pursuit
of His will, won't allow failure to be final.**

Contentment can be found
by accepting your current
circumstances while allowing
HOPE to bring you peace.

Ignorance, left untreated,
can result in full-blown
stupidity for which there is no known cure

You have no control over your skin color but have complete control of your character.

A successful outcome is never ac accident...
It requires a specific plan designed to
expose and eliminate failure.

Leaders who have a servant's attitude
are bound to succeed
You can guarantee your own success
by helping enough other people succeed

**A loss with character still
intact is always a win...**

**Untapped potential is
stealing from yourself**

Positive Outlook

**When you consider your old clunker
to be a Cadillac in progress.**

Just a thought to consider...

Where does "down" stop and "up" begin?

**How do you know for certain
what a feeling should feel like?**

**When things get out of focus...
simply refocus.**

When things get out of control...
over control
until they are under control.

If politicians were healthy but needy,
instead of wealthy and greedy,
our country would be in far better shape.

**Some folks lack continuity
between
words and actions.**

**Satan's tests
God corrects**

It is not enough to do things right
or doing the right things,
success is the result of continually
doing the right things right.

**Cleaning house never feels good
until company arrives.**

Progress meets a "dead end"
when you confuse
activity with accomplishment.

Solving Problems...

So often, too many people seem
to
have all the answers
yet
never provide any solutions.

**Everyone should learn to listen
at the
speed of right.**

HOPE...

ONE SIZE FITS ALL

**Be careful where you leave
your footprints.
Children are master trackers.**

It is possible that children
learn to "half listen"
from adults.

Children will believe more
what you show them
than what you tell them.

If adults could remain children,
we would eventually work
out our differences.

**Those who are wise are always
willing to learn from those
with experience.**

Diploma or Degree...

**A perfect start to finding
out just how much you
don't know.**

Learning in the classroom is necessary.
Learning from experience is lasting.

When you don't feel like singing,
sing anyway.
Your spirits will soon catch up.

**A house becomes a home
as soon as LOVE
comes through the door.**

Why is it

Every time we hurry,
it takes longer to finish a task?

**Who set the standard for
ugly or pretty
and how was it determined?**

At what age does OLD begin?

**True greatness will never be achieved unless
ego is replaced with humility**

One of the greatest attributes of a good leader
is not found in his/her abilities...
It is found by recognizing and utilizing
the abilities in others

**Omit one "O" and try
using God sense**

**If you find it difficult to "keep your chin up"
take advantage of the position and pray**

The practice of humility guarantees
the road to peace
and contentment while a
arrogance offers a freeway
to certain disaster

When preparation joins perspiration,
the marriage will succeed

There is ONE culture with guaranteed success...
It does not discriminate
Anyone can join

CHRISTIANITY

There are two times in life we struggle
to fit in...
Youth and Old Age

**People regularly pursue happiness,
when contentment should be the goal**

Life is a Gift

**The GIVER delights
when the gift is used as intended**

**Practice love as though someone's
soul depends on it
because it does**

Heaven is not a place
where perfect people
get to go
It is a place where
people are perfected
and get to live forever

To care enough to pray for someone
is thoughtful
To care enough to act is helpful
A combination of the two will be successful

**A wealth of knowledge is useless
if you keep it to yourself**

It seems people so often look for something
Free
Yet, **God's grace**, a Free Gift
is too often overlooked or rejected

**True character is easily exposed when
words escape the exit**

Consequences for every action

There comes a time when actions,
right or wrong
will either be rewarded or punished

What God designed is well defined to
serve a single purpose
Live your life on purpose for that purpose

It is in the quest for winning that integrity
either flourishes or dissolves

If life's tests cause you to fear...even doubt,
Be assured security is always near...
Trust in the ONE Who passed every test

**My prayer added to this book is that
you, the reader may gain some perspective…
and one or more of the
quotes will stimulate your
thoughts causing you to think and act
in ways that help others .
Every day offers opportunities for you
and I to positively influence to another's day**

Author: Kenneth Allen Patrick

Made in the USA
Columbia, SC
19 August 2024

40628054R00039